Contemplations & Sensitivities

Contemplations & Sensitivities

LAMENTATIONS | ENDEAVOURS | DESIRES
EXPLOITATIONS | EXISTENCE

Oliver W Barrett

Published 2008 by

Transience Publishing

TL
transience

67 Woodvale Road
Beaumont
Ballintemple
Cork
Ireland

A catalogue record for this book is available from the British Library.

ISBN 978-0-9558927-0-7

Printed and bound in Ireland by Watermans Printers Ltd

Cover design and layout by designmatters

Dedicated to my parents

For being the people you are
and for the constant encouragement.
My eternal gratitude to you both.

Contents

ONE. **LAMENTATIONS**

TWO. **ENDEAVOURS**

THREE. **DESIRES**

FOUR. **EXPLOITATIONS**

FIVE. **EXISTENCE**

ONE

LAMENTATIONS

Forever with your smile and gentle way,
Never a thought of mine to slightly sway,
For you'd fill all of me - a feeling complete,
And my love would grow and never deplete.

Now There's Just Me

On occasions many I sought that friend,
To enter a revered place to dwell,
On chances few and opportune,
My heart relented and for them I fell;
Being not of the complicated kind,
Albeit of myself this opinion raised,
On familiarity this challenged view,
Of this never would I ever be praised.

'Tis truth and calm no more I ask,
Obscurity a welcome bonus true,
Then let my love cultivate itself,
Not coerced or paralleled with you;
Text and fact can be easily confused,
Opposing from an opposite end,
To date my experiences actually reflect,
An entirely different scornful trend.

Within the alliance it is I so hesitant,
From vows so lovingly exchanged,
For a doubting memory or two or twenty,
Tarnished the trust 'n greatly damaged;
Not knowing what exactly is the best,
But the worst I felt in greater pain,
The futility when one settles for less,
A union formed that is without any gain.

So I'll resolve to focus upon my view,
On encounters juncture to vet more pure,
Daren't not waste further precious time,
In forming a bond unless I'm sure;
And with this the risk I surely run,
Of much solitary time in latter years,
For this I'd gladly and happily choose,
Than again draining the well of tears.

Not too far away in admiring you,
Let slip my feelings made known,
Refrained not from words so true,
Your mercy as fallen leaf was blown;
Now for you to flirt and idly play,
Me for you a bauble whenever want,
I shouldn't, but throughout all day,
There for you and refuse I daren't.

Sole partisan affair I believed to be,
Not known how it was you felt,
Beat missed upon whispered to me,
Contrary to cruel this blow you dealt;
Or rightly cruel a more apt rendition,
For now over you I do wildly muse,
In my heart composed pithy petition,
Next phase to route I greatly confuse.

Or nothing more should come of this,
The moment now sealed in memory,
Without knowledge can't say I miss,
But dreamt in day it be extraordinary;
So I'll take with me wherever I go,
Brief touch in hands clasped firmly tight,
Doubt it now anymore of you to know,
Not torment myself with events of might.

Darkened nights view the stars above,
Twinkling through light years of voyage,
In wonderment I ponder my course to rove,
Left to throes of fate or such similar adage;
For way far beyond the most distant speck,
Insignificant it appears of myself thus pitted,
In the Greatest garden a place each fleck,
In unity, both you and I never permitted.

Brought You Closer To Me

No suspecting moment when I casually turned
And in saddened eyes the embers burned,
Not this I wanted, instantly drawn to thee,
In days I'd embark,
Brought you closer to me.

The morn seemed shy, sunrise appeared late,
So eager for contact to determine my fate.
The date was agreed, each again to see,
Phase of time amiss,
Brought you closer to me.

Each evening of ten from that date forth,
Talk and silence were without fraught.
The day arrived, across many a sea,
Brief glimpse once more,
Brought you closer to me.

In dried arid land with scarcity the norm,
This place I'd live from you I'd torn,
Everyday in my heart, nightly your words set free,
My abating constraint,
Brought you closer to me.

In a sojourn of days, further East I'd go
And seek out you, first touch I'd know,
Your kiss was sweet, slight tremble in plea,
To hold you tight,
Brought you closer to me.

And on return to land of my humble birth,
In much learned mind of life and worth.
To see you again, of this I decree,
A love has kindled,
Brought you closer to me.

Years few drifted by, the bond grows tight,
In tantalising touch, each and every night.
Desire now stronger, to how much it'll be?
But this in my heart,
You're now a part of me.

In Transit

Arrive with bare minimum of lot,
Enough for the voyage so brief,
In terms of the greater plot,
From problems vast, a slight relief;

The cacophony and bustle abounds,
As matryoshka, this world nesting within,
Language alien, with varying sounds,
Degrees of fortune both bright and dim;

Sit and watch the world busily pass,
Or more accurately its inhabitants,
Tears of joy and sheer happiness,
Then others the grieving incumbents,

Creeds so numerous and so vast,
From minute glances so little to tell,
All carrying their own specific past,
Gladly I'd listen if a moment to dwell;

Each precious soul then on its way,
Never no more an encounter with them,
Passing through, just a shortened stay,
In part me, but to their own a precious gem;

Just like sand in the wind we're swept,
What lays ahead couldn't be determined,
For those I admired and over silently wept,
Farewell to you 'till thy journeys end.

My Heart Ceased Roving

Could you be my utmost desire to see?
In paces not many, still out of reach,
In silent demure, a tugging lure,
This freedom between an unwanted breach;
All of you I watched and already wretched,
As there before me and there without;
My love there seated, as, my heart bleated,
Glanced celestially again, what's this about?

In silence perturbed and gently unnerved,
Concocted civil task some bridge so frail,
To traverse canyon of conjured demon,
That any advance forward to sadly fail;
Her hand verse held, tripped me and felled,
My catalogue of rarity an implausible addition;
Already I knew her, without probing further,
Demoted my chore from heavy expedition;

On tipples receipt, we did finally meet,
Her voice the gentlest of an angel's cry,
Not of my world, couldn't be foretold,
Heaven then take me should there I die,
From bounded copy, I was eager to study,
As what for she was the word to read,
With watchful smile, 'twas no trial,
There all my yearnings, nothing did I need;

We excited at, the similarities that,
Joy for each of the world to us it'd bring,
She uttered softly, words so soon unlikely,
In blossom as the first flower of spring;
In my heart I'd pray, for this fateful day,
Yet 'tis fate is the force without control,
So fret not, fear not, worry not begot,
Again it may be I, to be, the unlearnt fool.

They Departed in Silence

Duration plenty had quickly passed by
And his love for her was so real,
The chosen night he would, but try,
Forever her heart from her to steal;
Careful thoughts and plans did ensue,
The location was carefully chosen,
Believing done all he could do,
Even believed in the answer be given.

Moreover any other night so special,
All the eventualities were duly covered,
Timing of the essence so very crucial,
Feelings many without being unnerved;
Impatience intervened just after main,
Blueprint shelved for now to move,
Incapable of further wait and strain,
The moment to her he'd openly prove.

Deftly and in clandestine withdrew,
Of silken and tapestry, a tiny case,
Discreetly uttered his love so true,
Immediate reply depicted on her face;
In proximity and there around,
A rippled construal of the scene,
Aghast in silence the briefest sound,
Resulting unease not meant to demean.

In preparation of the onerous task,
One critical detail treated in whim,
An oversight or too haughty to ask,
If indeed she did also love him?
So sitting in a state of total reprieve,
Both deeply and firmly in a trance,
And about recovered enough to leave,
Then finally, they departed in silence.

No Less It Shall Be

Once more and again your presence I see,
Brought to awareness encounter of chance,
Your words measured alone, a chapter no more,
In vault of treasures from which to reclaim,
All my senses for others you did so easily maim.

It's the sea of blue protecting your soul,
The allure in the simplicity of your way,
Poise at the moment and so gently eased,
Gallantry of one without knowledge to wear,
Never by my side, a poignant thought to bear.

You with another and I resounded the same,
Not the case so wondrous it'd truly have been,
Assuming of course you'd the least of cause,
In attending an assembly so small,
To explore possibilities or nothing at all?

Time takes us forth with eventual dispose,
No more existence and each other to sight.
In this fleeting instant from you I did learn,
Brief presence down here never complete or true,
'Till you take my hand and draw me to you.

So it's with sadness and regret and joy I endure,
All this from stumbling upon your being,
Lest it not be you then no less it shall be,
To allow another my heart to cherish and feel,
Yet I'd indefinitely wait if yours I could steal.

Never thy sight did fade from me and
More, it was your demeanour and closeted way,
A book sealed never a page to me was aired,
Little did you know over you I cared?
And wondered as to what your heart did feel,
No passage gained, nothing did you ever reveal.

Time about self has a mellowing effect and
Not the past, but the future and what is mortally left,
For now more true although never untrue did
You ever appear, and what once your eyes hid
Now a glint, previously never did I attest, reside
With tempting, as guard was momentarily put aside.

For the curiosity over you that I once held,
Is now being shared at a much later time, this
I did not expect, informed I'll be when,
Secretly you take me and not a minute before then,
Of what thoughts of mind and feelings from past,
Maybe no correlation, but a freshly moulded cast?

Upon another year curtains to fall and an end to put,
Bringing a closure to scenes of tragedy and glee,
As we gently thread our way with loss and gain,
Couldn't once in my life falseness pitifully feign,
The true feelings of my heart and clasp them within,
'Twould be an act of folly, and an act without win.

Fervently I'll wait as to what words to me you'll
Impart- maybe no semblance to what I think they'll be,
But already your time of me you've openly given,
And further encounter to be an error, us both forgiven,
No, not so, too much of your body was openly saying,
Accompanying words to kindle, I will be quietly praying.

The Beacon Beyond

Into a vicinity utterly new to me, brought
On by an uncertainty of what of me to be,
Albeit, be said, that it surmised to decree,
Plagued by apprehension and uncertainty,
From such prior moves no experience taught;

Ah, but upon alien ground a vision to extol,
Replaced anxiety and a curiosity did occur,
Occupation of heart and advance no further,
Or presently vacated and of longing from her,
Too early to tell, but not of me make a fool;

In patience I'll wait, knowledge comes my way,
Nothing to do, but my distraction to curtail,
To this task I must endeavour, dare not fail,
For untimely leakage, an awkwardness frail,
Imminence in journey, as never then could I stay.

'Tis Here I Began My Fortieth Year

At fifteen minutes past the morning hour of ten,
The bell tower rang out,
A cacophony shrill of chilling chimes,
On a lonely bench where upon rested solitary soul,
Looking upon the sleepy cove of Cavtat,
In inked scrawl I penned these lines;

In reverie 'tis here I began my fortieth year,
Faculty of mind in thought,
Soma in good fettle and holding firm,
I reflected on all doings on a life just over half,
But could not include a mate so worthy,
For her I did so desperately pine and yearn;

The sloping terracotta above homes did mind,
Below silently tethered,
The quay held affluence aloud,
In amity and in penury much smaller craft,
In slumber and obediently in westerly face,
Inert and alone I closely observed this alien crowd;

Higher again a steep ridge and natural protector,
Alignment for flying craft,
In defined slope gradually urged to the ground,
From where I know not, but each to their journey,
For some held treasures in love,
As for others some chance that this place not found;

Once again the echoing from the faces of four,
Snaps me away from pity,
And what I'd felt to be past rejection,
Carefully eyeing the cruiser again silently on its way,
In actuality never did experience the worst,
Indebted I now felt then altered my reflection.

You Are My Friend

You are my friend whence first so little known,
Our encounter was brief and within did ponder,
Yet in further forums on me you quickly grew,
We were of the one mind, seemed already knew;

You are my friend laughing at the simplest things,
And reasoning the workings of concealed powers,
In times of difficulty we turn and easily confide,
My respect and liking for you, never could I hide;

You are my friend and over you I quietly agonise,
That whatever misfortune to befall will be brief,
And with regrets so few and a life lived to full,
Yearning in my voice, tears in my eyes to dull;

You are my friend, daren't no more could I ask,
You've given me all that I consciously require,
In our friendship I hope that the terms were equal,
For to lose you a space, not in this life could I fill.

Two Slippers

An instant attraction it was for sure,
The form was so very pleasing,
Yet caution welled up from pristine,
And with me could she be teasing?

In script and in distant voice,
Noticed an inconsistency or two,
Not one edition did she relay,
Then left pondering on what was true.

Bother not in being bemused,
My soul not tendered, but in lusting,
No impediment in desiring to eagerly touch,
Damned if I'd be drawn into trusting.

Betrayed my mind with moral shift,
Happily played the lower ground,
And entwined, our bodies snugly fit,
Ecstasy in passion we easily found.

Touch so light and brushing glance,
The wanting surely never ignored,
Eagerly sought secluded grounds,
To allow each other be devoured.

Yet my wanting soul had its needs,
Not content with further rejection,
Niggled me away from the flesh,
A task riddled with much distraction,

Times patience and urge did wane,
As the taste eventually aged sour,
Traits of need did emerge,
And now no more do I see of her.

Memories many are engrained,
Some I'd gladly trade for free,
Lessons learnt when hearts relent,
For whom and what is to be.

Beside the bed a definite image,
An eerie reminder of life past,
Behind Two Slippers in silent repose,
For in that being I'd surely never last.

A Treasured Memory

Aren't thou the youthful lady girl,
Modern in look with a fashion twirl,
Cramped years into intuitive mind,
With compassion you treated me so kind.
Pined for have no doubt you'll be,
Moving onward novel facets of life and free,
Portion of my heart was so rightly captured,
At the instance of need and when it mattered.

Please do recall tea and the infrequent tart,
I know I've ceased this from being a part,
But a longing, a journey beckoned again once more,
With doubts a plenty drifting away from shore.
A memory faded yellow, as eventually all to be,
Forever a trace unforgotten, of this you'll someday see,
For as life permits and flight still in my being,
Often in my thoughts, only yesterday you I've seen.

No Regrets

Alas for the endearing man,
As he presented his case to her,
He couldn't offer her anymore,
Her mind just would not stir;

She refused time and again,
To the gallant advance he made,
For not a single one thing more,
Than the promise that he gave;

Her clock was ticking and wedding bells,
Reverberated around in her head,
But this he did not believe to be,
Crucial elements remained unsaid;

So what is it that dwells way down,
Hidden deep within her heart?
Why would she then go so far,
And then abruptly pull up short?

Confusing sure there is no doubt,
Reluctance to openness?
The man meant no harm and now,
All he's left is ponder and guess;

The refusal was graciously accepted,
And live with it he must,
The story would have been welcome,
But in him she just didn't trust.

A memory she said is what it is,
And a memory is what it'll be,
Yet barely a trace there now survives,
But wonderment in lives' diversity.

Lonely Old Man

Who is it you are my solitary friend?
Loneliness so sad I see in your eye,
Could I be wrong in my assumption of you,
Should I join you and listen or don't bother to try?
Your hands are strong from years of toil,
The clothes on your back ravaged from wear,
Witnessing your humbleness has tampered my heart,
Consuming a meagre bite, appearing without cheer;

Is it a home of silence later to which you'll return?
No companion waiting patiently for you to greet?
Did all of this pass you, no off-spring you have,
The love of your life, never the chance to meet?
I wish you well old man and my stranger friend,
May happiness invade and raise your spirit,
In the remaining days ahead I pray they will fill,
With much laughter and smiles and conversations of wit.

TWO

ENDEAVOURS

Oh it's all so very mad, but a necessary
madness in which to survive.

Life drains me-but then,
isn't that it's purpose anyway.

As youth quickly withers away,
And the mind moves on along its way,
Taking with it the mould now set,
And the devastation of prior years met.
Parity in balance to be the expected norm,
Brevity in wisdom exulted during days of storm,
To be fortunate and in receipt of good advice,
In near preparation for almost every vice.

On convergence of age the youth will be,
Well fancied and expected early to see,
Those of the wily and devilish sort,
Masquerading and on mission covert.
Confidence and much demure in talk,
Needless threat from which to easily walk,
In control of this sought and desired trait,
Masses covered, but for learning never too late.

Now images appear of the fallible being,
The past of suffering all too much has seen,
Boundaries weak, thus decisions poor,
A fool for all and the well disguised lure.
No hand to reach out to all this innocence,
Through the hands of models of incompetence,
Its not the place for I as from their own to learn,
For those in this failed role I do so angrily spurn.

How much more does remain?
And for how much more will I ever sustain, in idleness
From living or is the enigma in presenting,
Sure what I thought I'd unravel, to now I'm slowly consenting, nothing,
No path, no destiny for to comfort, possibly as one marching cohort.

For hesitance is of the mind,
As time's not an ally and of this you'll find, it cares not
And simply trundles along-in uniformity,
Albeit in stages it appears to drag in painful drudgery-but one thing
Its not and never it accuse, of being diffident, only yourself to ruse.

Opportune is a fleeting whim,
Lost in extended thought and thus without win, lest be in
Receipt of utensil weighted in sterling,
Or blessed with a wished upon star distantly twinkling, for most
Such will not be the case, dreams a plenty and for them to chase.

Whatsoever is the chosen pursuit?
Temporary postponement and the hallowed truth, an unknown
Limit placed on our bipedalism sublime,
From upright manoeuvres to being permanently supine-without
Life, but never the less, a unique existence of varying progress.

So as the creases of age slowly extend,
Wearing of parts to a stage without mend, all time to each
Will eventually be something no more,
And all shall not end in enlightenment, of this I'm sure, but hope
Breeds within the living, thus in its presence, never cease in pursuing.

Closed My Eyes

On closing my eyes to reflect on a past of whys?
And of all the many beginnings that have expired.
With some a smile creased, with others sense ceased
And of others still there is regret,
Over those on which my eyes did set,
With the natural draw never once have I tired.

Extended period they'd stay, then on their way,
Never delved deep enough thus no reasons came.
But I wonder in indolence, this never made any sense,
But permitting myself in candour,
My heart will once again strive for,
Another yet met and my wanting heart to tame.

With my eyes still closed, my humming mind still housed,
All things deemed trivial to the greatest of pains.
All unnecessary deaths, loss of fathomless depths,
Passing as All will eventually succumb,
Grief to the very point of numb,
No preparation to cope with indelible stains.

For all a hungered place, overly within wanton space,
Ravishment in moments if they identified so great,
Not let the time elapse, prior to friendships collapse,
Love and understanding over persons so dear,
Not at the intake of breath for the final fanfare,
For culpability will seed as then time too late.

My thoughts I tried train all but the present refrain,
Neither over my shoulder nor past the mountain see,
'Tis where I stand now, I'll work it out somehow,
Sanction for the present as tomorrow may never come,
Dare an adversity to think it I'll shun,
On finally closing my eyes this cooped up spirit to free.

I, one of many, and not entirely unlike you,
With a harboured treasure residing within,
Suppressed by reason and dormant for years,
Divestiture of binds and eradicate the fears;

Not all matured 'fore gift brought to bare,
Pastels of expression and watery oils,
Melodic concord for the perceptible sound,
In years not ten, the accomplishment astound;

For some that possess the calling unclear,
Triggers in life tempting talent step forth,
And rouse which ever it is that dwell,
Elating confidence, doubting self to quell;

In cocoon of the mind rejection no chance,
Works and effects trickle brilliance so great,
Then on exposure to soul, one other than thee,
Attesting the creation, for all else to see;

Time plenty has elapsed the present awaits,
Again, I say cast mantle permanently aside,
Objective of task neither for worship nor fame,
But Celestial bequests, from these don't refrain.

Fulfilment in Being

Of troubled past and of presence mislaid,
Eradicate forever from thought,
The future ahead prior to days no more,
Of missing out on happenings I'm fraught;

Should this thing I'm doing be my place?
Or that of man on distant green?
Maybe a cleft far away from all to see,
Enlighten my soul what does it mean?

Voracity, yes that may be the way,
And travels far over vast beyond?
Then with this I see complications so great,
Ever watchful of the crooked vagabond;

Or to take a love and my heart relent,
For her all I have and to provide,
But in one all my love peril for sure,
In time her roving eye and my heart divide;

Come now dispute not a newborn of gene,
A replica of thy self to see,
Therein persona not like any other,
I love thee child, but thou not complete me;

So auspicious is one to attain such things,
True great achievements they are,
Yet without daren't state that life unfilled,
Forging ahead would I not bother to care;

In my mind this nuisance unending persists,
Yet isn't the solution residing in being,
To have contentment evade dour and sadness,
About this place of state it'd be utterly pristine.

Run In The Rain

After hours in daily loathsome task,
I did go for a run in the rain,
To clear my head and heavenly ask,
Release from all anguish and daily strain;

I thought of all that I currently do,
No hindrance from which change to make,
And the possibility of all things new,
A weighted task from the present to break;

I fretted and battled deep within my mind,
Feared the darkened recess unknown,
With miles tread past the answer did find,
All troubles when sought had flown;

From the clouds the deluge drenched,
Erased my doubts and eased my pain,
For in salubrity, my future clenched,
Now the simple delight of a run in the rain.

A Sudden Sadness

Feelings from deep have welled up today,
Sadness has surprised me in a peculiar way,
Lost and sorrowful with remorse for life,
Cast away on my own this lonely night.
Desperately trying to see the brighter side,
My pact to keep and my promises abide,
I know what's right and what I've done,
Is all for the best, but still I'm forlorn.
I'm scared to think that I'll never fend,
And throughout my life always depend,
I reflect a lot on all that has gone on,
And think I'm stronger than what I am.
And of this sorrow and to take anymore,
Preventing peace within to spread galore?
I pray to God to give me the strength,
To challenge each and every event.
Now I'm sad and my heart is in pain,
In arms to cry and to right me once again,
This night again and to my Lord I'll pray,
That tomorrow will bring a brighter day.

Disenchanted

I'm so disillusioned, she did solemnly sigh,
No dare nor challenge in which to pry,
In its stead thoughts aimless and meandering,
Seeking pleasures and to them gladly surrendering,
But toils that soon lose their appeal,
Then beg and borrow from others to help one feel,
'Till finally folly or madness does invade,
Disregarding zest and letting it slowly fade,
Not this, I say, could I watch and silently observe,
But once again to you brimming full of verve.

Shadow of Darkness

Failing spirit careering upon a downward spiral,
Places to hide as all too much to accept,
Chillingly for the first, a shading to last,
Courage rescinds from a depth never to collect.
Ambling without aim with vision blurred and fogged,
No design to be seen, and if any, not much the gain,
The struggle grows daily 'n void of tempting,
No more veiled affliction and from others to feign.

To the duality of one I quizzed on how much to endure,
Would I recognise dementia should balance tumble?
Now supposed lucid thoughts and in mortality fixed,
The greater steadily grows every moment by the double.
Yet even in blackness pitch and all about rapt in fail,
From where I know not, one seed still contained life,
And in it all hope, an almost overwhelming task,
In time it'd spring forth and bring an end to the strife.

No simile nor metaphor of renown,
Scarcely depict my inner self,
Narrative an inaccurate portrayal,
Vast ponderings to meaning and fate,
Minute occurrences and happenings great.

Again yet another diary to safely hoard,
Entries depicting encounters per day,
Apiece the lines say the least,
But conjoined a life slowly to unfold,
Posting of the final period, never foretold.

Life not yet complete, happiness evades,
Lost in diversions that quickly wilt,
Riddance of the material distraction,
And in solace of my mortal remain,
Enchantment within, the answer attain.

My journey from now to alter course,
Enhance what's now just partially present,
And scour to fulfil ahead of providence,
The pieces hidden to complete the riddle,
To give and share and love where lovable.

A Most Necessary Transition

Somewhere along during the transverse of life,
Youth does surrender to adulthood,
And grasp the challenges presented forth,
To couple emotional survival with physical worth.

'Tis better to break away the motherly bond,
Sooner before the strut has strengthened,
Upon ones own to battle the daily elements,
Foundation sealed from ill poised torments.

It is not a matter of reckless abandonment,
On the contrary a compliment great,
That decamped youth now is well prepared,
For the ravages from which earlier spared.

Tasks great and small of regular occurrence,
Each dealt with in timely gain,
All the while striving to mature in outcome,
Sustainable in this world you have become.

Much thanks for the makers of thee,
Their role a resounding success,
And now what's left but your part to play,
In fitting and in instinct contribute some day.

Of unbearable days and hours to amend,
To engaging moments that I'd never want to end,
Labour and pleasure let them both copiously fulfil,
The wanting of mind and of vacant heart lying still,
Diversity 'n vigour to both not a moment too soon,
Not put resolve to the test, no never this to groom,
For there's a point lays beyond which is threadbare,
From whence task an enormity to about muster a care,
For many paths and temptations are littering the way,
Not always proud of conduct and the things I'd say,
I'll endeavour, I'll plea, I'll call to my deepest faith,
And in beckoned for reprimand to my very last breath,
Beneath the baking sun or darkened clouds of cold rain,
There're pools of emotions with plenty of smiles and pain,
Therein granted upon us this life so lovingly conferred,
Tempting whispers of quitting omit from ever being heard,
Being aware that life harbours the greatest of perils,
Prepared now for the best and the worst that it hurls.

The Obstacle Called Life

The sight that I used to behold,
As I wakened in the morn,
With a mind in a troubled shroud,
It was the rays of first light,
Unhindered by a single cloud.

For a time that has left me,
Pleasure I just cannot attain,
As Life events have built a wall,
Now against which I must face,
Retain motion or alas sadly fall.

With all at once I've tried to deal,
As if a single cluster attached,
But my heart bore so heavy,
Thoughts troubled twenty thousand,
Too many tasks borne with difficulty.

To overcome the obstacles ahead,
Was not to scale the single height,
But to take each problem part,
Thus treated and dealt with cast aside,
Mounting heap now upon laden cart.

Neglect not life's deterrents,
As mortar does harden fast,
Move on them well in time,
'Fore they get that chance to dwell,
And nightly with them you'll dine.

Not ill informed I believe we can cope,
To overcome the worst calamity,
Onerous it does appear believe,
But in division is where progress resides,
For the most I'm sure success achieve.

The Child of Today

In whaling you arrive and totally at mercy,
One of nature's quirks and simplicity of creation,
Needs so little during this critical of times,
Dependency great over the next few years duration,
Maybe those from whom you naturally descend,
For causes and choice take their leave of you,
Whatever to believe the decision thus made,
Through a riddled system you're assigned parents anew.

In the years ahead maybe curiosity will arise,
But in infancy now, love and care is all you desire.
Soon you will learn to crawl, smile and utter words,
And finally walking to get the things you require.
A body growing fast developing sinew and mass,
Becoming robust against the knocks of daily task,
And all the while your mind a sponge of perpetuity,
Absorbing everything and much of it you'll mask.

Intrinsic traits explained by the passing of gene,
And the nurturing I pray will be true and heartfelt,
Alas not all brought to bare in secluded uncertainty,
Kept way down within and no attention them dealt,
The experiences of then, the effects to later abide,
And those of models each as important as the other,
Their role and duty is to teach and love you right,
With confidence and trust with issues and bother.

Not long it'll be 'fore the child will have developed,
And its preparedness for life will hinge on rearing,
With the task complete and the resulting ventures forth,
To what lays ahead the past will in degrees be tearing.
The child of today will be the future of tomorrow,
And the time given to prepare is but for an instant short,
Now the cycle is due for yet another revolution,
Experience gathered to alleviate and reduce potential hurt.

Still I'm Longing

'Tis here I reside today,
What will be of me tomorrow?
Continuing in my heart,
There lingers some sorrow,
Sure causes there are many,
In this my very state of being,
Stemming from all I've heard,
And felt and of all that I'm seeing,
And of all possible eventualities,
My ever pondering restless mind,
From the good and bad I've endured,
To the utmost and the very kind,
No true meaning yet I've learnt,
It still does cunningly evade,
But of it I've searched knowing,
It wouldn't obviously itself parade,
In lonely seclusion, this
Mystery I will eventually figure,
Believing my questions of being,
Will rightly become even greater,
Resulting from this pursuit,
In time I'll have proof to attest,
That with true love in my life,
To much of this a welcome rest.

Days appear to unknowingly slip and time leisurely ticks away,
And upon this conjured concept, routines for ourselves we make,
Some for the sheer love of it, for the most I doubt another way,
Is the question wasted in knowing, that us it'll eventually take?

And to this regular pattern, an infirmity presented in severity,
A dramatic altering revealing, a mortal window presented clear,
What was once done in mundane, not considered now in brevity,
Much appreciation there is of time, every moment treasured dear.

Alas it'd take such an ordeal, for ones eyes to be teased,
The beauty of morning sun and in creation of seeds there sown,
Such loss and callousness upon ourselves, as in time we will be eased,
From this place of the living and permanently away from all we own.

*U*pon our path did we miss a turn?
An alternative route upon which to take,
Our most recent years a lesson realised,
Now learnt and a change in direction to make.

But is this not all just pre-empted fate,
Alterations are just part of the plan,
Every bob, weave and wrenching upheaval,
We'll endeavour to do the very best we can.

Life at times seems so very unreal,
Difficult to extract meaning at all,
A clutter of thoughts, too much to sense,
A distant cry, a familiar voice to call.

I should worry about it never no more,
Of it nothing positive did I ever see,
Invite soothing calm to a permanent place,
And convert what presently is to better be.

Once again a bearing and altered track,
For being too long in stagnant state,
Longing for completeness never abate,
Root not lost from the odd glance back.

Not all but some I did opine,
Not laying as prey to predator cold,
Enough the same from them be told,
Permit sought to print my rhyme.

In granting I did surely take pride,
The dotted line a familiar name,
And time not long first copy came,
Elation in success I couldn't hide.

No chance to lord on my haunches,
No spoils received with which to lodge,
No need at all from leeches dodge,
No signings or hectic launches.

It'll take not a compilation,
But on the cover alone my epithet,
'Tis then I'll see this dream be met,
In my death there'll live creation.

Not content and not yet achieved,
As another aspiration does reside,
Or two if you like side by side,
A most recent notion I conceived.

In dialogue of life depicted,
Enacted the players skilfully project,
The realism of the subject,
Patrons related to and captivated.

THREE

DESIRES

In a fleeting moment easily recognised
When yearning eyes fell upon and tantalised.

The Dutiful Drones

What more than the epitome of grace,
In elegance of gait and winsome in face,
No crier to announce, no fanfare loud,
Beyond the bounds of preventing a crowd,
Word like lightening so quickly to spread,
Murmurs and whispers, asking if she's wed?

To enhance the lure of the eager drone,
In garment brief and corporeal shown,
Enticing nectar, pollination in stealth,
Familiar surrounds never awkward she felt,
Yes, queues for this their queen to breed,
No advert required, for there isn't a need.

And busy about her, they joke and cajole,
Clowns without face they ply their role,
So silly they look, no conduct to resemble,
The quip of Creation conducting the ensemble,
In bids against others and thus be chosen,
Unleashed hair and about her shoulders there fallen.

With wariness in eye her courtiers screened,
Emboldened by tease of her skilfully preened,
Alas, no instant attraction, that first impression,
Difficulty in mind from frequent idle digression,
With stroking of hair and disarming smile,
For the pitiful pursuers 'tis an arduous trial;

All too familiar, now jaded, tedium the mood,
Of assemblage none over on which to brood,
Her part thus played, curtains soon to fall,
Impatience to alight despite beg, plea and call,
So a departing scheme, about time bid adieu,
And in politest of decree, none to follow you;

In unison, no rehearsal this scene to ever capture,
No spouse over consort could ever rightly censor,
They were left standing idly, cruelly moronic,
As the departing creature was akin to iconic,
Thus the queen will again, about a drone to find,
A wake of broken dreams scattered about behind.

Don't Turn Away

With thoughts plenty, none sombre too much,
In solitary of person, but my heart was in touch,
For time not long past, this I had easily believed,
Never cause had I felt, but myself I've deceived;

For an entrance so humble, just now she strolled,
A stranger to me and immediately her I extolled,
Across the near empty room, she sat duly with he,
Already I pined, for her not accompanied by me;

Distracted I felt and with no thoughts for my other,
Banished so easily, thus a need to undo the tether,
Is this what it takes to identify the process of settling?
Demons placed in my heart and now savagely battling;

Again I glanced over, preventing time from interfering,
And hoped beyond hope, now at a point without caring,
If she'd just cast an eye about her close by surroundings,
And maybe take some pleasure, from her meagre findings;

Not quite explained, isn't it exactly the thing she did,
About her she screened, with sentiments poorly hid,
Misconstrued so viable, but in her eyes resided pain,
Her longing was displayed only to break away again;

There quietly I sat and watched and lavishly admired,
Like a puppet propped up, inanimately never be tired,
Over and again when opportune my direction she stole,
And away from her courtier exerting to ply his role;

Time was quickly ebbing and an end seemed imminent,
A move hastened upon or forever myself to torment,
Scribbled note left with tender, an oddity of the game,
In heartened delight, hadn't she herself done the same.

A Healing Embrace

This night will you hold me tight?
In gentle embrace and sweet caress,
Soft hands in which to rest
And rid me of all this aching stress.

Brief utterance you know me now,
Just the calm and odour so sweet,
The rhythmic heaving of your breast,
All troubles lifted when bodies meet.

It's a passing moment to shortly end,
Of this I know it'll help ease itself,
A weakness now in which I'm suffering,
To end soon and again be myself.

Back on track to face the dawn,
Adhering to the few words you say,
And believing that my lot improve,
Looking forward again to the day.

Your magic once again sufficed,
Quelled the pain in mesmerising spell,
A tonic of worthy proportion,
Moments with you and now I'm well.

Should not lose sight of the gift
That I've received in the form of you,
Wonder how I could ever repay,
Tell me what it is I should do?

Soon the role will alas reverse,
In your eyes the pain reside,
And all you ask is to hold you tight,
Darkened moments be by your side.

Beauty So Rare

It is not my imagination vivid, in my minds eye I clearly see,
A collage of different images, the beauty that's best for me
The depiction that I've formed, of not just externally,
But made up of all her traits, she unlike any unequivocally.

Yes, I can see her clearly now, totally and completely unfazed
By her eloquent refinement, all too regularly I'm amazed.
Just to know such a person, an honour that I'd behold,
But contentment would quickly wane and her I'd want to hold.

My delirium would try her mildly, but not to the point of break
As she'd softly try to reason, citing the carnage in my wake.
Dealing with the depths of my lows, waters never too deep,
Together we'd sit in silence, talk and at times a huddled weep.

Not foolish enough to think that it's I the bedrock solid,
Without such a presence in my life, it would undoubtedly be horrid.
To this day the proof is there, my emotions a shredded heap,
But in my thoughts you are, your acquaintance I'd reverently keep.

An exuded subliminal message,
Imaginary words held high above,
   Bolding stating, man in waiting,
The wanting fool in plentiful grove;

Not I conned a thought believe,
Of handsomeness alone attract,
   Surplus tender, to surrender,
An honour to gift the finest carat;

My eyes to blinker from beauty,
Ulterior manner bears no semblance,
   To me, over thee,
Heart bruised from jousted lance;

On instruction to my weary mind,
Of accord to shy firmly away,
   From beauty, a pity,
'Tis an easy pact from which to stray;

The entente once again relaxed,
As beauty overshadowed my view,
   Oh dear, so clear,
The outcome shalln't be anything new;

To that which never fails to impress,
Upon me and my eyes dilate,
   Fight not, tangled knot,
One moment elapsed already too late;

I'll indulge when such visions I see,
Not resist the most natural thing,
   Desire it, court it,
For its not I us together bring.

Do You Think

Do you think we will continue just as we are,
Depending on chance for when next to see,
Do you think we could finally utter some words,
And add to our already widened eyes of glee.

Do you think the attraction is in all but one,
And in the sight of me you'd only just abide,
Do you think I'd not care to hear this you say,
For in truth your glances are impossible to hide.

Do you think it wise to let fate pave the way,
Letting weeks and months and longer perhaps,
Do you think this time was never meant for us,
Too long and eventually our interest will lapse.

Do you think its just an infatuation so brief,
I'm sure that you must be feeling the same,
Do you think each glimpse we wantonly steal,
The age old practice the primeval wooing game.

Do you think as in chess for me the first move,
A strategy so blurred in securing this date,
Do you think in curiosity you'd at least agree,
Shuffling of pieces in equality of mate.

Do you think now that it wasn't so bad,
In fact it was all that we did ever desire,
Do you think the quest now had its merit,
Each from the other now all we require.

Do you think now your choice was right,
I'll venture to preserve your initial thought,
Do you think and feel as I strongly do,
Reciprocated love as together we brought.

Over This I Muse

I'm tainted yet again by a creature so very fine,
Mind already playing the romance of some future time,
And then love, oh longed for love to creep in;
Further ahead a bond to grow so firmly tight,
At all days end with a gentle kiss to begin the night.

Then between us the gift of some issue few,
Beloved faces and semblance not entirely unlike you,
Swift days together to cherishingly count;
Contrived with such vigilance and such care,
But would it all in reality, to this even slightly compare?

A Beautiful Face

There is the one simplest
Of pleasures and this near
Always seems to be the case,
Troubles quickly packed away,
On sighting a beautiful face.

A cruel game nature plays
When beauty amongst our mist,
It's the perpetual gaze
And awkwardness to shame,
Thoughts are a labyrinth and maze.

A matter of confidence it is,
Such easy words to say,
Not for shy that quality without,
As the task becomes so heavy,
With seeds laden full of doubt.

Pedestal is where it's placed,
Way out beyond our cast,
At least this all in the mind,
Exquisiteness to remain at bay,
And approach may prove to be unkind.

But now I'm that bit older,
Many traits of before have faded,
But still my heart will race,
My eyes will brighten and ablaze,
On the sighting of a beautiful face.

She Knows Not How I Feel

Whence first I saw warmth in face,
And then shortly a voice ever so sweet,
My doubts so quickly did erase,
As my wanting love I did finally meet;

From where or what this I formed,
A prior opinion as to what she'd be,
But then that morning she gracefully roamed,
Oh please grant it Lord as her for me;

Never considered any sacrifice so great,
Nor even thought it a potential effect,
Patiently I'll wait and her words say it,
My desire approved and not to it object;

As for now she knows not how I feel,
Causes for this a complication of two,
Yet on knowledge of one I will reveal,
Time too much past to hide what be true;

I love to see her as there I silently watch,
And wonder of the sentiments within her heart,
And if feelings directed my way for me to catch,
The sheer elation of it all would near almost hurt.

Maybe Some Day

Someday maybe I might see you,
At a time that I'd least expect,
And in that instant of sighting,
Memories of none to recollect;

You know, never before we've met,
No trace, even of the briefest kind,
Not knowing you it matters none,
For you resided deep within my mind;

No evidence or reasons given sound,
No promise from high above,
But my heart does patiently linger,
Believing I've not missed out on love;

And true some encounters did befall,
Brief and extended some did endure,
But in resistance my feelings did hold,
Punished both as longing without cure;

Many loves maybe exist for many,
No chance there was this twist of fate,
In candid innocence there'd be only the one,
Yet, perhaps never I to happen upon this date.

FOUR

EXPLOITATIONS

Are their smiles in your heart?
Or an aching from which you'd gladly part?
I know such pain can suddenly sprout
Leaving you numb with feelings whipped about
Life like a paralleled universe, a distant world
Words to accurately depict have never been told
Like stepping-stones we do carefully thread
No land in sight just the oceans vast spread
But we cling to hope, deep rooted belief
Purpose and realisation and much sought relief.

Whence a threat is perceived by the diffident,
'Twould undoubtedly be only dewy-eyed fools,
That'd fail to see through the shrouded intent,
For within this treacherous plot there exist no rules;
Alas 'tis the forthright over this lacking do suffer,
Harsh punishment meted out in flagrant conceit,
Lest the naturally adept with that revered allure,
Imperil a fancied prominence and them defeat.

Shrouded mutterings galore denounce the travesty,
But none amplified within the vicinity of cause,
For during turbulent times there exists no certainty,
The necessity for each their own sanctuary to house;
And the solidarity of thought if it ever existed at all,
Now nothing more than the servicing of lips,
For some imminent egression others the awaited upon call,
An exodus so great of many one way trips.

The mystique astounds it remaining permanently within,
Over those embroiled and their much narrowed vision,
Does comprehension elude and perceive memories to dim,
Nothing gained from this other than heightened derision;
The outward track will flex returning in immeasurable chance,
Over the hallowed ground held by those unduly harmed,
Bringing with it the aggressors now to receive their penance,
For a mystical force intervenes for those so wronged.

What workings corrupt your head?
With deeds upon me to oppress,
And take from me my spirit free,
Why not leave things as they be?
With force you've encroached upon,
And entered my space of reverence,
My words of claim not matter to thee,
Resulting turmoil, not for you to see.

Beyond your understanding minimal few,
This thing to me brought without call,
One day, someday, strength within me,
Or cry to ally and upon you set he.
Never this, but now given choices scarce,
And an end to you as no more to cope,
Not I enslaved by your deeds deathly heavy,
Now at the hands of others without mercy.

No dream this is from which to wake,
A piercing whistle comes raining down,
Climatic change not of the weather,
As Ordnance is the ruler present,
Aged conflict erupts in vicious fury,
Land pot marked - so many to bury.

Annals silent collected stories of brave,
Hidden in troves forgotten long,
More of the same aching repetition,
Territory specific, a different place,
A need to reclaim land of heir,
Peacekeepers lost - dreadfully unfair.

Should nations united stand idly by?
On slabs their own cold in the sun,
Duty tours, yes as volunteer,
Risk for sure, death not considered,
Community at large need to mediate,
Quell the heat - ease the hate.

Is the diplomatic chair no longer seen?
Dialogue and case be heard,
Once man was revered in walking forth,
Conflict resolved in a different way,
Sheath the bloodied foil,
Agreement to reach - allot the soil.

No dream this is from which to wake,
Resonance in loss of life and limb,
Hearts tarnished forever more,
Minds bruised beyond repair,
And for what in our limited time,
A natural death - the final chime.

Brief Lapse into Sanity

A lull from the place deep within,
My mind on life did solemnly view,
Of ruthless acts, kindness in dearth,
Gripped my heart, shortened my breath,
Is this the world in which I grew?

Pain appeared the dominating trait,
Anguish a strong contender too,
Deceiving cheats and cunning lies,
All encompassing emotional cries,
Periods of joy appeared so very few.

What's this thing of lucid existence?
Sophisticated creatures supposedly,
Of much mayhem, slight evidence in care,
Brief helping hand, I'm just about aware,
Extortion, deals and crimes deathly.

Couldn't envision how I'd manage now,
Planets' orbit a demonstration of things,
Spinning wildly and in a greater ellipse,
All sanity from being will eventually eclipse,
Darkened days, await to what it brings.

All too much for me so again retreated,
Crossed the threshold for extended time,
Ruefully and solitary therein I'll remain,
From this world of yours I'll gladly refrain,
Your madness bares no resemblance to mine.

Not Christ's Mess

A bare solitary ten of moons so full,
Before tinsel and mistletoe again to see,
Once revered a Christian birth now so dull,
In its stead a festival of spending spree.

Brief tender touch of this there's plenty,
Yet no affection nor friendly glance,
But eyes trained, the glint is greedy,
Witless bustling executed in a trance.

Say it, what drives such endeavour?
Blamed on child of wanting taste,
A hidden ruse for such behaviour,
Transparency and words of waste.

It's the dark abyss of shallowness,
No substance at all there is,
Material splurge in unrivalled success,
Content on the pinnacle of ignorant bliss.

The luminous star above all to attest,
Guided a trio each with erudite mind,
To the humblest of all places to rest,
Fit for a King, yet united with animal kind.

And thereafter a life with possessions few,
Heart full of goodness and message to pass,
Letters and gospel and parables new,
In righteous living and no wrongs trespass.

The senseless and strain is not Christ's mess,
Set time aside and quietly reflect,
And assistance render to poor unfortunates,
Quietly bow on leaving, coupled with genuflect.

The Woman in the Window

$\mathbf{A}$ sphere of old yes 'tis true, but what of the choice?
No passing of judgement, of this I'd loathe and be hesitant,
Yet from enquiring mind and of you splaying upon another bed,
Consider options of a more humble approach in its stead?
In trepidation of this you may well permanently be wed?

Of hostility so easily plied from hands of the unforgiving,
Or on having been duped, nothing appeared as was hoped,
Then to soften the hardened with mention of distant family,
No semblance at all to your childhood dreams of destiny,
Daily the etchings tearing and scraping away at your dignity;

Spare a thought on a scheme for riches quick and great,
For this at its price and the enormity of the sacrifice,
And the accounted for past that surely in time will be denied,
For the truth to surface when unwanted you'll be petrified,
As it does from dormancy, the scoop then steadily and openly pried.

The Cost of Buoyant Times

Such furore there is during times of new,
Ostentatious spectacle for all to see,
A bogus surplus 'tis no mean feat,
To the debt collectors shortly meet;

An influx great from lands far and near,
To feed from the booming times,
Acute spike reaching skyward,
Abreast with activity totally untoward;

Surplus times are certainly here for sure,
Contrasting to the way of old,
Wealth was concealed and quietly hidden,
The present way is displayed in open;

This sudden mammon with pecuniary split,
A rift between the social classes,
The scale of penury is vastly mounting,
Charitable lists are quickly growing;

A policy firm is urgently required,
As sudden collapse is oh so imminent,
Before this mess becomes out of hand,
Who'll rise up and make a stand?

I fear none so great lives amongst us,
All immersed in individual enrichment,
Pockets rattle while on the make,
To right the wrongs what will it take?

So let us all sit back and watch unfold,
The demise of the growth so sudden,
As foreign corporatism sources new land,
Upon buckling crutches on which to stand.

*Y*es, true it stated that I made an acquaintance,
Nothing more or less did it occupy my mind,
Regular in way, as all in effort similarity of kind,
Our meeting had no cause at all for any pretence.

And thus it stayed, no wavering did I notice small,
All encounters were the briefest and little discussed,
Then movement in vacated being and opportunist,
Whence my slant tipped from balance and it did fall.

Whether ingenuous or unheeded unsure I am to say,
But in certainty my previous sense has dissolved,
For another I now see and not that earlier viewed,
The change as stark as night surrendering to the day.

When ascendancy bequeathed spare a thought to this,
The worthiness of benefactor for post thus allotted,
For in given power, this callous thus roams unfettered,
And grief inflicted upon those whose position is hapless;

Not all uniform in mode whence jurisdiction expanded,
Alas in command an altogether tale will sadly unfold,
This found knowledge could hardly ever be foretold,
Lesson not learnt, as such errors once again sustained.

Is this what we have become?
You and I so different,
And Vastly so,
The man coiled in the doorway,
Outstretched hand you shun to know;

Not content with your material toys,
And your wife to eye,
Showing you insist,
A perpetual parade of worldly goods,
What are you proving to me, why persist?

Is it the case of a fallacy great,
Grandeur in your thoughts,
You feel not,
Your lowly beginnings forgotten,
Nothing over all others is what you've got;

To argue this you naively challenge,
Pitch against wizened mind,
The void grows,
You fail to see beyond tangibility,
Onlookers with smirks and raised brows;

No more of my mind to you I'll impart,
Your greatness is profound!
I'm not being unkind,
You see, I know where you're going,
And exactly what you'll leave behind.

In You I Did Trust

At a moment so vulnerable
When friends were so very few,
Knowledge of a specific kind
I discreetly sought from you;
In this experience you showed
For me it was a first,
The land I tread was alien
And in you I did trust.

From that day I was told
On my instruction to thee,
That the process had begun
And my conscience to be free;
In your capable hands I left it,
You'd work hard and in earnest,
Never a moment did I doubt
As in you I did trust.

Many times you were asked,
'Was there any progress to date?'
I was informed that the system
Would surely have me wait;
With nothing at all to question,
Deceit was surely the furthest,
That notion never crossed my mind
For in you I did trust.

Now it transpires years later
After originally I first asked,
You did absolutely nothing,
Couldn't help but you I cursed;
The liaison has now evolved,
It's you the conceited purist,
I now pursue without choice,
Can't believe in you I did trust.

The Summer of Innocence Stolen

Close to half a score of years elapsed,
Youth marked with jokes a plenty,
And a mind that queried at length, which
Was a delight for the sibling foreign,
Who eagerly awaited upon innocent probe,
She the chosen guardian whence born.

Then the day dawned when all ceased,
No more childish scrawl arrived,
A loss in heart for the exiled one,
Which naively misconstrued, did see
The natural progression in life,
And not as it later turned out to be.

Now in darkened hours and thoughts,
The innocence lost did struggle,
With not knowing of the sullen mood,
That had now become the norm.
Just over a single score again, the
Time taken to face into the storm.

Persons dear and close were told,
Resulting in much shock and tears,
And anger towards the taker, well
It was nothing more than expected,
But the proper path be taken,
And not another, but respected.

Justice and servitude was delivered,
The shackled taker was led away, but
With no relief as was anticipated.
Never it emerged and a hand to lend,
It seems now the damage done,
No length of lifetime could it ever mend.

FIVE

EXISTENCE

Of all the uncertainties, it should be in knowledge of the one certitude that would have us influenced to excel to our fullest potential, whatever that may be. Time is not ones ally.

For one not to be engaged in a livelihood of gratification is akin to odious sustenance, survival won't be threatened, but neither will it be very pleasurable.

My Abiding Companion

That bit closer you've encroached upon me today,
Yet hesitated and allowed me my eyes to open,
For this day and others, beside me, please do stay,
Not nearly prepared for the Next, me to be taken;
Not enough attained, there's so much to explore,
Youthful years with vast eagerness for things anew,
Accompany me, please not intrude, you I implore,
My destiny to find, with mishaps I'm sure a few.

Not half in expectancy and still in anxious search,
Others not this choice, taken in a guise of ways,
Diversions from me, my time from you to stretch,
And motivates my pursuit to fully utilise my days;
Just after lunch now in this palpable imagery of life,
More learned, yet striving further, a place believed,
Accepting that time will deliver some grief and strife,
And pain brought about from those who've deceived.

Early evening, the light is weak and appears faded,
Your attention on loved ones, from me, them you took,
Tears of loss, but joy as no more into the lives they lived,
Your presence so close, grasped me and mildly shook;
Strive on and endeavour like a whisper firmly in my ear,
Whatever thy persuasion, thou faith, whatever its sort,
On a list compiled, not ordered, informed I do appear,
Decision made, hence the search not long, but short.

Existence does wane, indications, body that's much aged,
It's quite late for me now, should retire for the day,
Of the chances, the risks some of which were hedged,
Remorse over regret, I'll learn to cope, nightly I pray;
No love on this earth powerful enough for this prevent,
My departure, it's the necessity of years that have past,
Further no more, life clinging to a body that's well spent,
Ah, my abiding companion, your attention on me at last!

Conviction of the Resident Within

For Cormac

Where are you now, the bravest of the brave?
Carried your burden, with a smile to the world,
Always sparing with time, so much mirth within thee,
You know, of your roguish face forever and always I'll see,
But with the advancement of time the severity unfurled.

Throughout all waking hours from reminders no rest,
And to essentially assist as without this you're composed,
Your breath was short and thereby struggled to breathe,
To have a pulmonary procedure was your critical need,
An offer of semblance to quality and an extension disposed.

To undergo this needed exchange criteria to meet,
No strength within thus heavy reliance on tabular form,
What of this synthesis and development to lastingly cure,
No progress from mammoths, no enticing lucrative lure,
The suffering and agony continued from the time whence born.

To bear witness to the ravages forever my mind to haunt,
Of its grasp upon you no chance were you ever allowed,
Life gradually squeezed and painfully it was curtailed,
For ever your courage as a reminder, it to be reverently haled,
All pain finally ceased and thou returned to earth so hallowed.

Come and Go As You Please

To close my eyes in dreamy thought,
And take my mind from you,
There is nothing for me to prevent,
From doing what you'll always do.

The timing of your arrival,
This I can determine with accuracy,
On occasions your mark to leave,
And it's done with total complacency.

Such drama you're prone to cause,
At specific times of the month,
Terrible heartache and earnings lost,
Your mass I'd dearly like to shunt.

The peculiar thing I find with you,
Is your generosity beyond a fault,
Many mouths you cause to feed,
At this I wouldn't ever dare to baulk.

Another trait you bring such delight,
To the aged and children in awe,
The shrieks of heightened excitement,
As slowly towards them you claw.

Yes, it's true you combine it well,
Providing something for everyone,
Be it when you decide to rise,
And then later when you're gone.

Your greatness is one of much talk,
At times an analogy of you I use,
And for always there'll be you in my life,
In sombre and also when you enthuse.

The Garth That Is Martina's

*U*pon a road that I no more than never,
Travelled between two familiar spires,
Thereto a dwelling with shutters green,
With walls of lime and a plot of treasures;
The eyes that so lovingly surveyed,
A plan hatched for the intended look,
Therein beds lay strewn, as if no order,
No garden path this, none never she took.

Almost nature alone the force to model,
Pollination as each species claims its patch,
And harmony as not seen in any other,
On limited space, fresh soil to eagerly catch;
In a perfumery laid wild in which the air to fill,
The aromatic fragrance of lavender and rose,
In refraction each glance reveals a subtle change,
Colours of contrast and akin carefully chose.

In a planted sense 'tis a peculiar thing,
A Cottage Garden whose appearance is wild,
As if seeds and bulbs were randomly strewn,
The natural look, more the dabbling of child;
But in this place, beauty is captured in many forms,
In sight and smell, intoxicated from shortened stroll,
With eyes closed, easier the gardeners heard,
Their unrelenting buzzing, with the wind they toil.

In stepping out the door and for years depart,
Leaving your charges to their very own devices,
They'll not disappoint on your return to view,
No better you'd have done than all their choices;
It's inherent that order can go against the grain,
Nature has a course with the slightest of nudge,
And no better example than this garden I see,
More than a brief assist it'd gratefully begrudge.

This stimulus is to me the least,
Of bitter and sweet no loss in try,
A drop, a nibble or a stately feast,
But for sustenance, no fare for I;

Forests garden during summer rain,
Nature's odour permeates the air,
The intoxication of vixen vain,
Alluring scent of maiden fair;

The haunting note of curlew high,
Fury in pitch of roaring typhoon,
Of sweetened whisper unto die,
Innocent cry of youthful scion;

Upon me your hand softly place,
Moistened lips I beg gently press,
Then tenderly to stroke my face,
Tantalising me you finally kiss;

Fabulous steppes and prairies vast,
Ranges high and canyons deep,
Of thou the very finest cast,
Your beauty all to covet and keep;

Of this no sense it defined to be,
Yet without no senses elucidated,
Each sense in peculiarity,
And to how they are translated.

What If

What if I was from a different place?
With vastly different things to do,
And what if our paths never crossed?
And you never saw my face;

What of a life lived so simple?
Without peak and dip endure,
What if no chances ever took?
And no peril to invite and meddle;

What if without years growing old?
No wrinkles and grey to show,
What if it's all suddenly curtailed?
There still in state and growing cold;

What if in immortality write?
No more than it to leave behind,
And it for ever me remembered by,
No difference to me to have got it right;

What if I now finally accept?
That from others a difference small,
And to cease questioning into what if,
No right have I acclaim to ever expect.

Upon Coiled Paths

*U*pon coiled paths we definitively do slide-
'Round and 'round till from this earth divide,
No cosmetic tampering decline the rate,
Not lest evolution set the trend, with
minute altering to which we obey
and ever so slightly extend the decay;

To withdraw and within secluded space,
Seated and opposite an identifiable face,
Observe in miniscule the oldness set in,
'Twould hardly be noticed at all, thus
we shalln't squander our cherished days
with unnecessary acts and trite delays;

But given a memory vivid or crumpled image,
A comparison to draw against face to envisage,
Down upon shrivelled hand with gentle tremble,
Acts of ease never given much thought,
Replaced by effort and much deliberation,
The crux of life and its natural devastation;

What of a reprieve for an extended spell,
An eternity granted on this geoid to dwell,
Would takers many avail of this bequest,
Dare no thought given to resulting cause,
For sacred reasons or believers different,
Adequately full it can be more than sufficient.

All Do Depart

Albeit umpteenth courses and many bearings to steer,
Uncharted waters filled with doubt and anxious fear,
Within each an intrinsic force not that of equal ability,
Some attaining utmost rule alas for most lowly majority;
Others then with features that grace media so many,
Consider the trauma resulting from those of tyranny,
Or lives of solitude as those giveth their life to prayer,
Forces of war and peace within situations of danger,
So of the ways and endeavours towards which us draw,
Filling us with love and experiences that ravage us raw,
To the ultimate whereby without choice we do depart,
Bid farewell in parting ceremony, for believers a new start.

Time To Go

In confidence it can be foretold,
Diminished activity of life so full,
And, in time, my mind to pitifully dull,
In advancing years as I grow old;
In good fortune 'twill be the case,
Neither forward nor back to look,
Suddenly, or not, my ability took,
And all I can do painfully erase;

Not death could I ever deny,
Vision to see me there laid out,
This state I would eagerly tout,
If nothing no more could I ever try;
In not being able in every task,
From first moment in the morn,
My heart wretched and tearfully scorn,
Aid from another it necessary to ask;

Such an existence I'd never abide,
Reliance on others in daily chore,
My senses would, surely, quickly bore,
My disinterest in being never hide;
So solemnly I'll have you know,
When my mind and body denote fail,
Father, my suffering soul please hail,
For me at least it'd be time to go.

AUTHOR'S
NOTES

The author wishes to acknowledge the following publications by Forward Press & Poetry Now in which earlier versions of some of the poems appeared:

Restless Soul, *Love Conquers All*, *Déjà Vu*, *Life's Wonders*, *Awakening Inspiration* and *Lifes Serenity*.